Made in the USA
Columbia, SC
07 October 2024

43781965R00062